# *21 Days to Free*
## DEVOTIONAL JOURNAL
*A Drama Free Blueprint Presentation*

Copyright © 2020 L. Chanel Thompson
All Rights Reserved

www.LChanelThompson.com
www.TheScatterBrainedGenius.com

Cover Design © INKBlot Media, L. Chanel INK
www.LChanelINK.biz

Unless otherwise stated, all noted Scriptures have been taken from the New King James Version (NKJV) of the Holy Bible.

No portion of this publication may be reproduced, stored in any electronic system, or transmitted in any form or by any means (electronic, mechanical, photocopy, recording, or otherwise) without written permission from the publisher. Brief quotations may be used in literary reviews.

ISBN 978-1-7338696-8-3
LCCN 2019911884

This devotional journal is dedicated to

*Dr. J. G. McCann, Sr.*

The Man of God and The Master Teacher who inspires me to purposed living...

# Introduction

You know, forgiveness is one of the most powerful things in the Universe. I believe that's why God tells us in His Word to do it, practice it, study it, apply it and ultimately...live and die for it. It's not a physically "die" for us, but it is definitely a spiritual and mental death to whatever already happened. God intended for us to live FREE from anything that was sent directly from Him. That alone set me free, a bit. But I had to take it a step further. What good is being forgiven by the God of the Universe and not by ME?! Did that hit you like it me? He can wipe me from existence and instead, he chose to set a full 400 year plan in motion before I was even thought about being born just to FORGIVE ME. I need you to really catch this so you can be healed and operate in your full freedom. The **Key** is that you have to apply forgiveness to YOU first. You have to receive it from God through Jesus, the Christ, and then you have to, you have to, you have to...you have to APPLY it to yourself first. It's just like *Faith* without works is dead, *Forgiveness* not applied to yourself is dead. He gives it to you FREELY and so we are to give it away to others FREELY! Now let me just briefly say what freedom is NOT. It is NOT doing whatever you want, whenever you want, however you want to whomever you want. Nope, that's NOT Freedom. Freedom is actually having the ability and the capacity to do that and...wait for it...choosing NOT to do any of it, but instead choosing to do what you know is RIGHTEOUS according to the Word of God.

*Introduction- Ground Zero*

Forgiveness has become almost synonymous with weakness. It's not a word used widely in common conversations and it certainly has never been the buzz word in my personal lifetime, but I've found it to be one of the most powerful freedom corralling principles a person can ever learn and apply to their lives. Listen, as you age, yes, you will be more cognizant of wanting less and less drama in your life – you will do some maturing and "settling". I'm just here to get you FREE way before and even if you never settle due to aging. I'm excited that you decided to be courageous and take this 21 Days to FREE journey with me, practicing DAILY how to forgive, forget and flourish living a life of healing, peace and freedom.

The Devotional Journal Journey is outlined in 3 Sections where we will walk through the practical application of Forgiveness and living Drama FREE: *7 Days to Forgive YOU, 7 Days to Forgive THEM,* and *7 Days to Forget and Flourish*. Each Day, we will:

- ✓ Study a Blueprint Level – a person in the Bible who operated in forgiveness and that includes God the Father and Jesus the Christ.
- ✓ Learn a little bit about the background of the Scripture and an application of forgiveness to our daily life situation, the Excavation; and
- ✓ Pray and Write about (journal) on how we applied it, the Foundation Strategy.

It's simple, but it's deep and I want to help you apply it to your life. So let's get started on this 21 Days to FREE Journey! I will see you at FREE!

# Ground Zero – The Foundation

## Daniel's Prayer

3 So I turned to the Lord God and pleaded with him in prayer and petition, in fasting, and in sackcloth and ashes. 4 I prayed to the LORD my God and confessed: "Lord, the great and awesome God, who keeps his covenant of love with those who love him and keep his commandments, 5 we have sinned and done wrong. We have been wicked and have rebelled; we have turned away from your commands and laws. 6 We have not listened to your servants the prophets, who spoke in your name to our kings, our princes and our ancestors, and to all the people of the land. 7 "Lord, you are righteous, but this day we are covered with shame—the people of Judah and the inhabitants of Jerusalem and all Israel, both near and far, in all the countries where you have scattered us because of our unfaithfulness to you. 8 We and our kings, our princes and our ancestors are covered with shame, LORD, because we have sinned against you.

*19 Lord, listen! Lord, forgive! Lord, hear and act! For your sake, my God, do not delay, because your city and your people bear your Name."*

Key Verses: Daniel 9:1-8; 19 New International Version (NIV)

## Excavation

Ground Zero is all about the vehicle in which we will use to get FREE: **PRAYER**. Prayer is not be taken lightly – it is the only way to communicate with God, to hear from Him and to get heaven to respond to God's will on Earth - this is how you activate your angels to lighten your task in the natural. In order to begin this journal journey to DRAMA FREE, you have to BELIEVE that prayer is real and serious and that it works. *Daniel* teaches us some keys about prayer. I always say it like this: "my vertical alignment has to be straight before I can do anything else." Vertical ALIGNMENT is a critical *Key*, prayer, your belief in its power, is critical to our successful journey.

Daniel's prayer is INSTRUCTIONAL as is the Disciples prayer[1]. Daniel answers all the "Q"s that good writers, and powerful prayers use. Daniel gives us a clear portrait of prayer and devotion. He lets us know WHAT happens WHEN I need direction from Heaven? WHERE do I need to pray? WHERE do I need to send this Heavenly help? WHO, WHAT, WHEN, and HOW do I do this? This is the strategic transformational power of prayer to make REAL changes not only in the heart of man, but also in the Earth.

Another *Key* to Ground Zero is ensuring that you can you take your personal relationship with God and ask Him to bless someone else. Abraham did it with Lot[2] (Sodom and Gomorrah), Moses did it with the children of Israel[3], Daniel did

---

[1] Matthew 6:5-15
[2] Genesis 18
[3] Numbers 24

*Introduction- Ground Zero*

it for Israel in bondage, and Jesus, the Christ did it for eternal humanity. Remember that getting FREE, living FREE and staying FREE will keep you thinking of others. Let's begin.

## Daniel teaches us WHO?

Daniel STARTS with himself. He puts on sackcloth and ashes and makes up his mind to posture himself to pray. By the time he is done, he is able to pray for an entire nation, but he started within. That is where we start – **ourselves** – the YOU in the situation. He did NOT start any of his petitions with I or me, He used "we" throughout because he knew that this was bigger than himself. He knew that was he was praying for was to cover generations after him. This journey to DRAMA FREE is about your freedom and that of everyone connected to you.

## Daniel teaches us WHAT?

He clearly discusses, through confession and admission, the SINS that he needs God to address: *Rebellion* (v. 5), *Deafness* (v. 6), and *Shame* (v. 7-8). Daniel prays specifically and he prays for ACTION. That's how you get FREE – by SPECIFIC ACTION. We are going to take time to address our own issues before we even look at anyone else during this journey to DRAMA FREE; and we are going to take ACTION to get it done.

## Daniel teaches us WHERE?

He was specific and intentional on where he wanted God to send this heavenly assistance – where he wanted the action to take place. We will take care each day to be specifically directional in where, what areas, we want assistance in our journey.

## Daniel teaches us WHEN?

Well, this may be the most obvious, but we want to be FREE...NOW! Freedom from the bondage to UN-forgiveness is way overdue! After we pray, we should be EXPECTING from Heaven. We should be watching, listening and hearing what God's response is to our prayer! Daniel is very specific in his expectation. He says HEAR, FORGIVE, HEARKEN, DO, DEFER NOT - these are all ACTION words. And immediately, Daniel receives from God. God sees, He listens, He hears and He RESPONDS (v20-27)[ii]. We want a "suddenly" jail break like Paul and Silas had in *Acts 16:25-26*[4]. We will get free DAILY.

## Daniel teaches us HOW?

The specificity of Daniels prayer in the Key Verse relies on who God says He is; it reverences Him; it rededicates Daniel's life to Him; it outlines Daniel's faith in God; it refers Him back to His Word; it defines the outcomes in advance. Admission is the first step to FORGIVNESS. *Hebrews 9:22* tells us that *"without the*

---

[4] **25** And at midnight Paul and Silas prayed, and sang praises unto God: and the prisoners heard them. **26** And suddenly there was a great earthquake, so that the foundations of the prison were shaken: and immediately all the doors were opened, and every one's bands were loosed.

*forgiveness of sins there can be no REMISSION [removal] OF SIN".*[5] Daniel acknowledges three things that we all-all-all have been guilty of: Rebellion, Deafness (to God), and Shame. We are going to be specific every day of this journey to DRAMA FREE.

## Foundation Strategy

This first foundational strategy is critical to your journey. Here's where the rubber really hits the road. You are deciding, after reading the introduction that you will take 21 days of your life to change some things about the rest of your life. ARE YOU READY?!

Today, I want you to write out a prayer of confession and repentance based on Daniel's prayer example – MAKE IT PERSONAL. Be sure to focus on these aspects of the mechanics of your prayer:

**Did you start out with acknowledging inward and then upwards before OUTWARD?** *Remember to always get YOU straight FIRST. Get your VERTICAL ALIGNMENT first.* **What PRONOUN did you use when you wrote out your prayer?** *Remember that you will start out with "I" and once you are straight, you can move to "them".* **Did your prayer leave room to SEE, LISTEN AND HEAR God?** *Remember that prayer is a sign of faith and that we should always seal our prayers with EXPECTATION.*

---

[5] And according to the law almost all things are purified with blood, and without shedding of blood there is no remission

# Introduction - Ground Zero

# 7 Days to Forgive You

"Forgiveness is a gift you give yourself to celebrate your freedom."

*L. Chanel*

## Blueprint Level 1

14 Hezekiah received the letter from the messengers and read it. Then he went up to the temple of the LORD and spread it out before the LORD. 15 And Hezekiah prayed to the LORD: "LORD, the God of Israel, enthroned between the cherubim, you alone are God over all the kingdoms of the earth. You have made heaven and earth. 16 Give ear, LORD, and hear; open your eyes, LORD, and see; listen to the words Sennacherib has sent to ridicule the living God. 17 "It is true, LORD, that the Assyrian kings have laid waste these nations and their lands. 18 They have thrown their gods into the fire and destroyed them, for they were not gods but only wood and stone, fashioned by human hands.

*19 Now, LORD our God, deliver us from his hand, so that all the kingdoms of the earth may know that you alone, LORD, are God."*

**Key Verse:** 2 Kings 19:19, New Living Translation (NLT)

## Excavation

There are rules and conditions to this thing. You CONFESS. You ASK for forgiveness. You GET forgiven and healed. You GIVE forgiveness. YOU get blessed. Forgiving YOU is the most important aspect to operating in forgiveness – in my opinion. Let's see how someone in a high position handled forgiving himself:

*King Hezekiah*. Hezekiah was a good king, I mean the Bible does not refer to him as wicked, but he had some issues following God's instructions for his people AND he had a fear problem[iii]. But the one thing King Hezekiah did have, was the faith to believe that God could and would help him if he would just ASK. Sometimes it's just that simple. Forgiving YOU will require you to ask God to help you! It will require you to ask God to teach you HOW to forgive YOU like He forgave and continues to forgive YOU. That thing blessed my whole life. King Hezekiah ACTS out his petition for forgiveness by taking the actual letter from the enemy and laying it out in the temple – the same temple that he took the gold to give to the enemy trying to fix the problem of his fear! Now, I don't know about you, but that's how repentant I am. I go right back to the scene of the crime and ask God to get me straight! That's **Key**. He already KNOWS, so there is no need to hide it or flee the scene. And when we do so honestly, God will send a Word and a take care of our enemies.[iv]

## Foundation Strategy

Today, I only want you to think about two people: You and God. I want you to think about your relationship with God – whatever it is or not – and then I want you to say: *Father, Forgive ME and help ME to Forgive ME. In the Name of Jesus. Amen.* That's it. When you've said that simple prayer, I want you write down all the things that you think you need to forgive YOU for and then *turn the page*. Whenever you feel yourself slipping into self-condemnation, just repeat this prayer, add to the list and then *turn the page* again – as many times as you need to.[v]

7 Days To Forgive You

*7 Days To Forgive You*

## Blueprint Level 2

1 Jacob looked up and saw Esau approaching with four hundred men. Jacob divided the children among Leah, Rachel, and the two women servants. 2 He put the servants and their children first, Leah and her children after them, and Rachel and Joseph last. 3 He himself went in front of them and bowed to the ground seven times as he was approaching his brother. 4 But Esau ran to meet him, threw his arms around his neck, kissed him, and they wept. 5 Esau looked up and saw the women and children and said, "Who are these with you?" Jacob said, "The children that God generously gave your servant." 6 The women servants and their children came forward and bowed down. 7 Then Leah and her servants also came forward and bowed, and afterward Joseph and Rachel came forward and bowed. *8 Esau said, "What's the meaning of this entire group of animals that I met?" Jacob said, "To ask for my master's kindness." 9 Esau said, "I already have plenty, my brother. Keep what's yours." 10 Jacob said, "No, please, do me the kindness of accepting my gift. Seeing your face is like seeing God's face, since you've accepted me so warmly. 11 Take this present that I've brought because God has been generous to me, and I have everything I need." So Jacob persuaded him, and he took it.*

Key Verse: Genesis 33: 8-11, Common English Bible (CEB)

## Excavation

Forgiveness is so powerful that it not only frees YOU, but it absolutely frees **all involved**. Here it is with *Esau* and *Jacob* - the first recorded twins in the Holy Bible. They should have been close as can be, but one decision to deceive, lie and steal changed all of that. So much so that Esau, the older twin, who had been wronged, sought to kill his brother. And we already know that UN-forgiveness KILLS. But after many years, Jacob has been transformed by God and is returning, with his entire family, to make amends...to ASK FOR FORGIVENESS. Now that's a *Key* part to Forgiving YOU. You have to get the courage to ASK – first from God and then, if the Lord instructs you, from the person. When Jacob decides to ask for forgiveness from his twin, he EXPECTS to be killed and his children enslaved by a hate filled sibling, but what he finds, is a long lost love that was tainted by a lie and a brother who offers not only forgiveness freely, but wants to bless his brother's life. That's what self-forgiveness will do!

## Foundation Strategy

Forgiving YOU requires that you acknowledge the part that YOU played and no matter how small the "percentage", even if it was as simple as the way that you handled it. I am reminded of Moses striking the rock instead of speaking to it like God instructed and he missed out on entering the promised land[6]. Deep, but simple.

---

[6] Numbers 20:6-12

You have a part to play and that's the part you need to forgive. Today, I want you to think about the littlest of things that you may have done or failed to do that have ultimately caused you pain – just simply say what is. You know you say, "I knew I should have never…" or "Something told me to…" – yeah, that's the thing we want to uproot today. Let's pray: *Father God, help me to release every decision, every conversation, every action or inaction to YOU that you may cast it into YOUR seas of forgetfulness. I know I may never be able to truly delete it from my memory bank, but I believe that you can uproot the emotion that's attached and heal me permanently from the unforgiveness I've given to myself. In the Name of Jesus. Amen.*

Whenever you feel that memory being recalled, just write it down and *turn the page*.

*7 Days To Forgive You*

*7 Days To Forgive You*

## Blueprint Level 3

*Anyone you forgive, I also forgive.* And what I have forgiven—if there was anything to forgive — I have forgiven in the sight of Christ for your sake, in order that Satan might not outwit us. For we are not unaware of his schemes.

Key Verse: 2 Corinthians 2: 10, NIV

## Excavation

True repentance means to turn away from – 180 degrees. You are no longer facing the same direction. You are no longer headed down the same path. That's freeing. To know that no matter which direction you are facing, if you acknowledge God, confess your issue and ask for forgiveness, He will cause a turn (to the right direction) and then allow your life to be made new. Even if you've been removed from the church building, you cannot be excommunicated from the God who forgave you. Well, that's how forgiveness is supposed to work too. You forgive, you allow the person receiving the forgiveness, in this case YOU, to turn 180 degrees in the opposite direction and be FREE. Listen, if you are really going to walk in forgiveness, you have to operate in the TRUE repentance of it. You cannot walk in the same direction, live the same way, rehearse the same hurts. You've got to turn away. That's what Paul was telling the church – forgive these people and let them walk in repentance and FREEDOM in Jesus, the Christ.

## Foundation Strategy

Today, I want you to think about turning away from whatever it is that has held you bound up until now. Acknowledge it so that when you say this prayer and affirmation, you will turn and be FREE. Let's pray: *Father, You are so awesome in your wisdom that you knew I would need you to let this go. You knew that I would get to a place that the burden of it would get too heavy for me to go any further. I have held this thing against ME long enough and I want to be FREE. I drop it right here and I turn away from it. Help me never to reach back unless it's to help someone who is stuck there. In the Name of Jesus. Amen.*

Now, write it down, and pray that God turn every word, emotion, weight of it into a powerful testimony that will set someone else free...oh, and *turn the page*!

*7 Days To Forgive You*

7 Days To Forgive You

# Blueprint Level 4

## *Solomon's Prayer of Dedication*[vi]

22 Then Solomon stood before the altar of the LORD in front of the whole assembly of Israel, spread out his hands toward heaven 23 and said: "LORD, the God of Israel, there is no God like you in heaven above or on earth below—you who keep your covenant of love with your servants who continue wholeheartedly in your way. 24 You have kept your promise to your servant David my father; with your mouth you have promised and with your hand you have fulfilled it—as it is today. 25 "Now LORD, the God of Israel, keep for your servant David my father the promises you made to him when you said, 'You shall never fail to have a successor to sit before me on the throne of Israel, if only your descendants are careful in all they do to walk before me faithfully as you have done.' 26 And now, God of Israel, let your word that you promised your servant David my father come true. 27 "But will God really dwell on earth? The heavens, even the highest heaven, cannot contain you. How much less this temple I have built! 28 Yet give attention to your servant's prayer and his plea for mercy, LORD my God. Hear the cry and the prayer that your servant is praying in your presence this day. 29 May your eyes be open toward this temple night and day, this place of which you said, 'My Name shall be there,' so that you will hear the prayer your servant prays toward this place. *30 Hear the supplication of your servant and of your people Israel when they pray toward this place. Hear from heaven, your dwelling place, and when you hear, forgive.*

Key Verse: 1 Kings 8:30, King James Version (KJV)

## Excavation

Forgiving YOU enables YOU to do what YOU are purposed to do in spite of your origin story. Do you know that no matter what the situation of your birth is, if you will forgive you – even for being born – and submit to the purpose of God, he will bless you to be a blessing and do something tremendous! Let's see what happened with *King Solomon*, born into some serious DRAMA. The Scripture is his prayer consecrating the temple. So, that's the first thing; God chooses Solomon, in spite of his origin story of being born to adulterers, to BUILD HIS FIRST, OFFICIAL, PERMANENT dwelling place – THE TEMPLE. The temple that the Lord told his father, King David, that he could NOT build. Although King David had God's *heart*, he also had bloody *hands* and that disqualified him. God allowed David to have a second son by his mistress who became his wife – Solomon – and the Bible declares that the Lord "loved" Solomon. Not only did God *love* Solomon, but He *chose* him and ensured that he had everything he needed to complete the task. That's freeing to me and I hope it is to you. To KNOW that no matter what, God has already given you everything you will ever need to do what He purposed you to do; and that no one else has what you have! Solomon had only asked God for wisdom and in return God answers his life with wealth and a worthy purpose.[7]

## Foundation Strategy

Today, I want you think of the circumstances of your birth. What you do know and even the questions you may have or the utterly unknown. Know that there are

---

[7] 2 Chronicles 1:8-12

many people in the Holy Bible, God's Word that He chose to use mightily even with their DRAMA filled ORIGINS. Moses, Joseph, Solomon and even Jesus, the Christ, all had DRAMA in their origin stories and they each did great things FOR God and WITH God. Let's pray: *Lord God, you are the author and finisher of our faith. You knew us before we were even formed in our mother's womb[vii] and you still hand selected me for a divine purpose. I thank you for looking past my past and seeing me as my future, purposed filled self. I ask you to help me do the same. In the Name of Jesus. Amen.*

Now, go to the mirror and say – I no longer curse the day I was born, but I bless the day I was born because I have a purpose to fulfill!

Let's journal about our origin story and then...you know what to do...*turn the page*.

7 Days To Forgive You

*7 Days To Forgive You*

## Blueprint Level 5

23 And when Abigail saw David, she hasted, and lighted off the ass, and fell before David on her face, and bowed herself to the ground, 24 And fell at his feet, and said, Upon me, my lord, upon me let this iniquity be: and let thine handmaid, I pray thee, speak in thine audience, and hear the words of thine handmaid. 25 Let not my lord, I pray thee, regarding this man of Belial, even Nabal: for as his name is, so is he; Nabal is his name, and folly is with him: but I thine handmaid saw not the young men of my lord, whom thou didst send. 26 Now therefore, my lord, as the LORD liveth, and as thy soul liveth, seeing the LORD hath withholden thee from coming to shed blood, and from avenging thyself with thine own hand, now let thine enemies, and they that seek evil to my lord, be as Nabal. 27 And now this blessing which thine handmaid hath brought unto my lord, let it even be given unto the young men that follow* my lord. **28 I pray thee, forgive the trespass of thine handmaid: for the LORD will certainly make my lord a sure house; because my lord fighteth the battles of the LORD, and evil hath not been found in thee all thy days.** 29 Yet a man is risen to pursue thee, and to seek thy soul: but the soul of my lord shall be bound in the bundle of life with the LORD thy God; and the souls of thine enemies, them shall he sling out, as out of the middle of a sling. 30 And it shall come to pass, when the LORD shall have done to my lord according to all the good that he hath spoken concerning thee, and shall have appointed thee ruler over Israel; 31 That this shall be no grief unto thee, nor offence of heart unto my lord, either that thou hast shed blood causeless, or that my lord hath avenged himself: but when the LORD shall have dealt well with my lord, then remember thine handmaid. 32 And David said to Abigail, Blessed be the LORD God of Israel, which sent thee this day to meet me: 33 And blessed be thy advice, and blessed be thou, which hast kept me this day from coming to shed blood, and from avenging myself with mine own hand.

Key Verse: 1 Samuel 25:28, KJV

## Excavation

*Abigail,* King David's second wife, did not start out that way. David was her **second** marriage. Her first marriage was to what Scripture calls a fool. Abigail could have stayed stuck in the fact that she was married to a fool, but instead, she forgave herself for marrying him and enabling his foolish behavior; and then she took action and saved everyone. That's what forgiving YOU does: *allows you to help others who may not even know they need to be helped.* I can't go through it all here, but suffice it to say that her husband's entire camp was fat, dumb, and happy with his leadership and had no idea that his decisions were going to get them all killed, but God had planted a seed of forgiveness in Abigail that ultimately saved them.

Forgiveness comes with a measure of WISDOM. We know that because we just finished talking about King Solomon, the wisest man to ever live and we see that exemplified here with Abigail who used it to save everything connected to her. Her ability to forgive was so powerful that King David gives God praise that her actions saved him from shedding more blood! How real is THAT?! Oh, and that fool of a husband? God took care of him for her and she did not have to ask or pray or do anything!

## Foundation Strategy

Today, I want you to think about someone whose DECISIONS have harmed you, whose leadership may be endangering your well-being or the well-being of others. I have one on the tip of my thoughts at all times! Now, we are going to pray:

*Father God, I ask you to infused me with the forgiveness that brings WISDOM. I know that I am not all-wise, but You are omniscient, all knowing, all seeing and all wisdom comes from You. I thank you in advance for giving me Your wisdom, and for allowing me to freely use it as I walk in a life of forgiveness. In the Name of Jesus. Amen.*

Now, that we've prayed for the wisdom that comes with forgiveness, let's journal about what areas of our lives we can use it immediately and help someone who may not even know they need it! Oh, and yes, let's *turn the page*!

*7 Days To Forgive You*

# Blueprint Level 6

## Solomon's Prayer of Dedication[viii]

22 Then Solomon stood before the altar of the LORD in front of the whole assembly of Israel, spread out his hands toward heaven 23 and said: "LORD, the God of Israel, there is no God like you in heaven above or on earth below—you who keep your covenant of love with your servants who continue wholeheartedly in your way. 24 You have kept your promise to your servant David my father; with your mouth you have promised and with your hand you have fulfilled it—as it is today. 25 "Now LORD, the God of Israel, keep for your servant David my father the promises you made to him when you said, 'You shall never fail to have a successor to sit before me on the throne of Israel, if only your descendants are careful in all they do to walk before me faithfully as you have done.' 26 And now, God of Israel, let your word that you promised your servant David my father come true. 27 "But will God really dwell on earth? The heavens, even the highest heaven, cannot contain you. How much less this temple I have built! 28 Yet give attention to your servant's prayer and his plea for mercy, LORD my God. Hear the cry and the prayer that your servant is praying in your presence this day. 29 May your eyes be open toward this temple night and day, this place of which you said, 'My Name shall be there,' so that you will hear the prayer your servant prays toward this place. *30 Hear the supplication of your servant and of your people Israel when they pray toward this place. Hear from heaven, your dwelling place, and when you hear, forgive.*

Key Verse: 1 Kings 8:30, KJV

## Excavation

Ok, we need to go back to *King Solomon*, the wisest, the wealthiest, and the one chosen by God to build His earthly dwelling place. Remember in Blueprint Level 4, we talked about being chosen in spite of our origin story? Well, it gets even deeper. God has already said that He would visit the iniquity, the sins, of the father all the way to the third and fourth generations. Now, in human years, that could be 120 years or so if we give each generation 40 years! But, I love the grace and the forgiveness of God because He really KNOWS ALL.

Now, God did not want bloody hands – hands that had shed blood, hands that were guilty of murder, hands that had not been consecrated – to build His temple. Although King David, Solomon's father, was a man after God's heart, his hands were a filth of blood – righteous and unrighteous. So here, we see Solomon using his wisdom and his teachings about the things of God ensuring that he PUBLICLY acknowledges all the sin he can think of so that God can forgive it BEFORE anyone enters the temple! I wish I was preaching instead of writing right now! So, forgiving YOU is INCLUSIVE. It goes all the way down your DNA and geneology. Remember, Solomon was truly "born in sin and shapen in inquity" so his wisdom allowed him to go to the ROOT and cover it all.

## Foundation Strategy

Today, let's think about our personal genealogies. Let's think about what we KNOW and what God has revealed to us. I can think of many generational curses that I have had to identify and curse so that my children were not born under them. I want you to think of those things. Now, Let's pray: *Father God and Righteous Judge, we thank you for never changing your standard. By remaining consistent and never changing, we only have one standard that we need to follow and that is of your Son, our fully perfect, fully righteous example. I ask you for forgiveness for things that came with my bloodline, my DNA, my geneology – things that I had no idea were in me. In the Name of Jesus. Amen.*

Now, if you can, write those broken generational curses down here and let's *turn the page!*

7 Days To Forgive You

*7 Days To Forgive You*

## Blueprint Level 7

*For the director of music. A psalm of David. When the prophet Nathan came to him after David had committed adultery with Bathsheba.*

1 Have mercy on me, O God, according to your unfailing love; according to your great compassion blot out my transgressions. 2 Wash away all my iniquity and cleanse me from my sin. 3 For I know my transgressions, and my sin is always before me. 4 Against you, you only, have I sinned and done what is evil in your sight; so you are right in your verdict and justified when you judge. 5 Surely I was sinful at birth, sinful from the time my mother conceived me. 6 Yet you desired faithfulness even in the womb; you taught me wisdom in that secret place. 7 Cleanse me with hyssop, and I will be clean; wash me, and I will be whiter than snow. 8 Let me hear joy and gladness; let the bones you have crushed rejoice. 9 Hide your face from my sins and blot out all my iniquity. **10 Create in me a pure heart, O God, and renew a steadfast spirit within me.** 11 Do not cast me from your presence or take your Holy Spirit from me. 12 Restore to me the joy of your salvation and grant me a willing spirit, to sustain me. 13 Then I will teach transgressors your ways, so that sinners will turn back to you. 14 Deliver me from the guilt of bloodshed, O God, you who are God my Savior, and my tongue will sing of your righteousness. 15 Open my lips, Lord, and my mouth will declare your praise. 16 You do not delight in sacrifice, or I would bring it; you do not take pleasure in burnt offerings. 17 My sacrifice, O God, is a broken spirit; a broken and contrite heart you, God, will not despise. 18 May it please you to prosper Zion, to build up the walls of Jerusalem. 19 Then you will delight in the sacrifices of the righteous, in burnt offerings offered whole; then bulls will be offered on your altar.

**Key Verse:** Psalm 51:10, NIV

## Excavation

If there ever was a model for "forgive YOU", it is *David*. David was about his FORGIVENESS BUSINESS and he always started with HIMSELF. He is referred to as a man after God's own heart, even though he made a lot of mistakes. The one that He never makes in all of Scripture? Harboring un-forgiveness. He never mars his heart with the chains and bondage that failing to forgive brings. This entire *Psalm 51*, one of my core Scriptures for my personal faith walk, is about getting right with God and with himself. He does all the things we've talked about for the previous six days: He acknowledges his part by seeing it the way God sees it; He requests forgiveness from His God; He turns away from the place where he is never to return. That's something else to point out. There's not a lot of "and David returned" in his life, very similar to Joseph. Once they had an experience and moved from a place, that was it. I've often asked myself personally why I was disinterested in "reunions" – class, school, professional – because I just don't get excited. And this journey regarding forgiveness is my answer. Once I've "been there, done that", I drop it and look forward to what's ahead, even if the experience was good!

## Foundation Strategy

Today, we are going to seal SELF forgiveness with a special prayer:

*Father God*

I believe that you loved me so much that you wanted to forgive me and that you intricately planned my forgiveness and my soul's salvation. I believe that through your Son, Jesus, the Christ, I have been saved from the sin, the bondage of un-forgiveness and the weight of vengeance. I drop it all at your feet today and ask you to replace it now with PEACE. Your peace passes all understanding and I expect to be transformed by the renewing of my mind about FORGIVENESS. It was so important that you took thousands of years to create this plan to forgive me and now I repay that deb by choosing to forgive ME. I thank you for this transforming power!

*In the Name of Jesus. Amen.*


You can feel free to come back here anytime to renew your dedication to Forgiving YOU any time. Now... *TURN THE PAGE!*

7 Days To Forgive You

*7 Days To Forgive You*

# 7 Days to Forgive Them

"If forgiveness was not important, God would not have required His Son's blood to render it".

*L. Chanel*

## Blueprint Level 8

1 Then Miriam and Aaron spoke against Moses because of the Ethiopian woman whom he had married; for he had married an Ethiopian woman. 2 So they said, "Has the Lord indeed spoken only through Moses? Has He not spoken through us also?" And the Lord heard it. 3 (Now the man Moses was very humble, more than all men who were on the face of the earth.) 4 Suddenly the Lord said to Moses, Aaron, and Miriam, "Come out, you three, to the tabernacle of meeting!" So the three came out. 5 Then the Lord came down in the pillar of cloud and stood in the door of the tabernacle, and called Aaron and Miriam. And they both went forward. 6 Then He said, "Hear now My words: "If there is a prophet among you, I, the Lord, make Myself known to him in a vision; I speak to him in a dream. 7 Not so with My servant Moses; He is faithful in all My house. 8 I speak with him face to face, Even plainly, and not in dark sayings; And he sees the form of the Lord. Why then were you not afraid To speak against My servant Moses?" 9 So the anger of the Lord was aroused against them, and He departed. 10 And when the cloud departed from above the tabernacle, suddenly Miriam became leprous, as white as snow. Then Aaron turned toward Miriam, and there she was, a leper. 11 So Aaron said to Moses, "Oh, my lord! Please do not lay this sin on us, in which we have done foolishly and in which we have sinned. 12 Please do not let her be as one dead, whose flesh is half consumed when he comes out of his mother's womb!" *13 So Moses cried out to the Lord, saying, "Please heal her, O God, I pray!"* 14 Then the Lord said to Moses, "If her father had but spit in her face, would she not be shamed seven days? Let her be shut out of the camp seven days, and afterward she may be received again." 15 So Miriam was shut out of the camp

seven days, and the people did not journey till Miriam was brought in again. 16 And afterward the people moved from Hazeroth and camped in the Wilderness of Paran.

Key Verse: Numbers 12:13, NIV

## Excavation

The Lord can always intervene when necessary and He does. I thought about it, and one of *Moses'* more intimate family situations shows us. Moses had a speech impediment so I am sure that arguing with his siblings would have been very challenging. I also know that Moses was a fighter – remember what he did to that task master in Egypt? Yeah. It's time like those, when those closest to you, even someone like Miriam who once watched over your safety, is now speaking against you to your face. So, what do you do? NOTHING. You let the Lord Himself deal with the matter. I'm by no means saying that it's EASY, I'm saying that is very possible if you want to be free from what comes AFTER you take emotionally charged, unrighteous, angry, or vengeful action against another person. You just become a slave to an event for the rest of your life until you FORGIVE THEM.

## Foundation Strategy

Today, we're gonna hit home, literally. Many times, the first "un-forgiveness challenge" come from those that know us in the most intimate of ways, those who have our noses, those who have the same last name: FAMILY. Quiet as kept, the quicker we learn how to forgive those who are right in our faces, the quicker we'll learn how to LIVE A LIFE of forgiveness. Let's pray: *Father God, I know that you gave me the family that I have and you have been there every step of the way. I release every word and deed that has hurt me from someone who I deem as family. I ask you to uproot the emotion attached to it and that you allow me to walk, from now on, in forgiveness towards them...even if they never say "I'm sorry" and even if they are no longer with us. In the Name of Jesus, Amen.*

Now, write their names down here and one or two words on what they did or how they wronged you that caused you to walk in un-forgiveness and *turn the page*!

*7 Days to Forgive Them*

7 Days to Forgive Them

## Blueprint Level 9

12 So his sons did for him just as he had commanded them. 13 For his sons carried him to the land of Canaan, and buried him in the cave of the field of Machpelah, before Mamre, which Abraham bought with the field from Ephron the Hittite as property for a burial place. 14 And after he had buried his father, Joseph returned to Egypt, he and his brothers and all who went up with him to bury his father. 15 When Joseph's brothers saw that their father was dead, they said, "Perhaps Joseph will hate us, and may actually repay us for all the evil which we did to him." 16 So they sent messengers to Joseph, saying, "Before your father died he commanded, saying, 17 'Thus you shall say to Joseph: "I beg you, please forgive the trespass of your brothers and their sin; for they did evil to you."' 17 **Now, please, forgive the trespass of the servants of the God of your father."** And Joseph wept when they spoke to him. 18 Then his brothers also went and fell down before his face, and they said, "Behold, we are your servants." 19 Joseph said to them, "Do not be afraid, for am I in the place of God? *20 But as for you, you meant evil against me; but God meant it for good, in order to bring it about as it is this day, to save many people alive. 21 Now therefore, do not be afraid; I will provide for you and your little ones." And he comforted them and spoke kindly to them.* 22 So Joseph dwelt in Egypt, he and his father's household. And Joseph lived one hundred and ten years.

**Key Verse:** Genesis 50:17; 20-21

## Excavation

Have you ever forgiven somebody FOR REAL and they don't believe it? Here's how *Joseph* dealt with that. He was leaving the land and his father was dead, but his brothers who had put him in a pit and traded him for silver and lied about it all and kept the secret - they knew the power of the blessings that was on his life and they got scared...again. Now, if the truth be told, so many years had passed that everyone should have forgotten all about it. God had blessed everyone abundantly. Enough time had passed that mentally forgetfulness should have set in, and yet, here we are. 10 fully grown men are shaking in their boots about meeting their past in a different form of punishment and pay back. Sometimes, the hurt is so deep, the deed is so despicable and the torment is so vicious...BUT God. For all that negative, God had sown enough positive into Joseph that he only held love and forgiveness in his heart for his family once lost; even the brothers who set his whole life course into motion. And his love and his forgiveness was enough to make them believe it AND receive it. That's the true power of forgiveness.

## Foundation Strategy

Today, let's think about a hidden, untouched place...a place that we thought the "time heals all wounds" would fix, but it did not. Are you there? Good. Now, let's pray: *Father God, I thank you for showing me the root cause of my pain and my unforgiveness. I ask that you would infuse my mind and my heart with love for those who may have done me wrong and caused me pain. Lord, I confess that I really don't want to let it go, but I trust YOU enough to love them and YOU enough to forgive them and trust you for* the outcome – FREEDOM. I believe you alone for the return on my forgiveness investment. In the Name of Jesus. Amen.

*7 Days to Forgive Them*

*7 Days to Forgive Them*

# Blueprint Level 10

5 Now Adonijah, whose mother was Haggith, put himself forward and said, "I will be king." So he got chariots and horses ready, with fifty men to run ahead of him.

28 Then King David said, "Call in Bathsheba." So she came into the king's presence and stood before him. 29 The king then took an oath: "As surely as the LORD lives, who has delivered me out of every trouble, 30 I will surely carry out this very day what I swore to you by the LORD, the God of Israel: Solomon your son shall be king after me, and he will sit on my throne in my place." 31 Then Bathsheba bowed down with her face to the ground, prostrating herself before the king, and said, "May my lord King David live forever!"

**Key Verse:** 1 Kings 1:5; 28-31, NIV

## Excavation

Forgiving those in your family who wanted what you were ultimately given – just how is that possible? Those fueled JELOUSY, ENVY, GREED, and MAL-INTENT who have the same blood as you? What do you do? These are not people who you can easily cut ties with or that you want to be in constant conflict with, but you know that you can't just ignore the situation. *King Solomon* has our answer. He was indeed the baby boy – the love child of adulterous parents – his father just happened to be a King. He was given everything a Prince could want and much like Joseph, he was his father's "favorite". So much so, King David announced and conferred the throne to Solomon while he was still living just to make sure it went smooth. But that did not get Solomon out of his forgiveness duties. Nope, he had to make a decision for himself if he would forgive his brother – it was a private decision that Solomon chose to make very public, ultimately freeing himself from all the negative talk about his conception and birth and setting him up to create a NEW legacy based on wisdom and forgiveness.

## Foundation Strategy

Today, think about your blessings that came from pure FAVOR. These particular blessings were simply because you were favored and someone chose for no apparent reason, to bless your life. Now, think of someone, because there is always at least one, who was mad because they thought they should get what you got. They even claimed it...you got it? Now, let's pray: *Father God, you are awesome and all-knowing* and I thank you for never giving me what I deserve. You are all powerful and command blessings upon my life that no one can take away or take credit for. I say thank you today. Allow me to consistently and completely forgive those who despised your blessings and favor in my life. I give them over to you and ask that you would bless them too. In the Name of Jesus. Amen.

*7 Days to Forgive Them*

*7 Days to Forgive Them*

## Blueprint Level 11

13 His soul shall dwell at ease; and his seed shall inherit the earth. 14 The secret of the LORD is with them that fear him; and he will shew them his covenant. 15 Mine eyes are ever toward the LORD; for he shall pluck my feet out of the net. 16 Turn thee unto me, and have mercy upon me; for I am desolate and afflicted. 17 The troubles of my heart are enlarged: O bring thou me out of my distresses. **18 Look upon mine affliction and my pain; and forgive all my sins.** 19 Consider mine enemies; for they are many; and they hate me with cruel hatred. 20 O keep my soul, and deliver me: let me not be ashamed; for I put my trust in thee. 21 Let integrity and uprightness preserve me; for I wait on thee. 22 Redeem Israel, O God, out of all his troubles.

Key Verse: Psalm 25:18, KJV

## Excavation

How do you forgive others? *Forgive yourself.* How to get forgiveness from God? *Ask and then practice forgiving others.* I am in constant awe of how God creates synchronous interdependencies for His children to follow. We are all interconnected and interdependent no matter how hard we try to be independent. You can have a 1 to 1 relationship with God, but you cannot live this life alone. Even God's divine purpose for your life requires the involvement of others. God said it was not good for [hu]man to be alone and He meant it. Forgiving them is living the life of freedom AND reciprocity that God intended. The catch, the *Key,* is that you need to stay in constant communication with and confession to God.

## Foundation Strategy

Today is all about confession. Real Talk with God. You and God know all about who you have failed to forgive. You and God alone know the "THEM" who still hold the keys to your freedom to live a life of abundance and joy and Drama FREEDOM because of un-forgiveness. We don't even have to think too hard or long. Let's Pray: *Father God, I have failed to forgive and you know it. I have failed to confess my failure to forgive in the past, but I stand here today, ready and willing to forgive everybody and anybody who wrongs me, who offends me. I ask that You would honor my confession today and give me the fortitude, focus and faith to forgive. I trust you to make the wrongs against me right. I ask you to help me to forgive more easily, more quickly, more readily as walk away from offense and walk towards freedom. I trust your Word with my whole heart to vindicate me as you see fit and to forgive me swiftly as you promised. In the name of Jesus, Amen.*

*7 Days to Forgive Them*

*7 Days to Forgive Them*

## Blueprint Level 12

12 Then the Lord said to Moses, "Stretch out your hand over the land of Egypt for the locusts, that they may come upon the land of Egypt, and eat every herb of the land--all that the hail has left." 13 So Moses stretched out his rod over the land of Egypt, and the Lord brought an east wind on the land all that day and all that night. When it was morning, the east wind brought the locusts. 14 And the locusts went up over all the land of Egypt and rested on all the territory of Egypt. They were very severe; previously there had been no such locusts as they, nor shall there be such after them. 15 For they covered the face of the whole earth, so that the land was darkened; and they ate every herb of the land and all the fruit of the trees which the hail had left. So there remained nothing green on the trees or on the plants of the field throughout all the land of Egypt. *16 Then Pharaoh called for Moses and Aaron in haste, and said, "I have sinned against the Lord your God and against you. 17 Now therefore, please forgive my sin only this once, and entreat the Lord your God, that He may take away from me this death only." 18 So he went out from Pharaoh and entreated the Lord. 19 And the Lord turned a very strong west wind, which took the locusts away and blew them into the Red Sea. There remained not one locust in all the territory of Egypt.* 20 But the Lord hardened Pharaoh's heart, and he did not let the children of Israel go. 21 Then the Lord said to Moses, "Stretch out your hand toward heaven, that there may be darkness over the land of Egypt, darkness which may even be felt." 22 So Moses stretched out his hand toward heaven, and there was thick darkness in all the land of Egypt three days.

**Key Verses:** Exodus 10:16-19

## Excavation

Do you know when someone is genuine in asking for forgiveness? More importantly, do you care? Is the other person's sincerity relevant? Well, let's ask *Moses*, former Prince of Egypt. Here he is, deliverer of his people after 400 years of slavery and he's being confronted with a request for forgiveness. And he knows it's insincere. And yet, he forgives and stops the plague. Now this is remarkable to me because he's in the middle of trying to get deliverance, meting out plagues and here is this intimate moment and opportunity for us to see how forgiveness really works. It's really not about the other person. This is NOT to say that we don't operate in wisdom and obedience to God after. Clearly, Moses continued his assignment to deliver God's people up to and including the plague that killed the first born son of the man that he just forgave. God was fully aware that when He instructed us to forgive, that the enemy would make it difficult. God knew that the enemy would ask amiss. God already knew too, that He had a plan of eternal forgiveness that is so powerful that we just need to tap into it to live completely free in this present life. If you want freedom, you've got to take control of the situation by operating in forgiveness - unconditionally.

## Foundation Strategy

Today, I want to think about someone who asked for forgiveness and they were not sincere. We know that they were not sincere because their actions did not change after. They attempted to do the same or worse after. And yet, we forgave – the first offense – yet we are still holding onto their unchanged "after" behavior. Well, it's time to forgive that! Let's pray:

*Father God, You are so wise and Your ways so far above our ways that no matter how we try, we will never be able to fully comprehend them. So, we come to you today to ask for your spirit of UNCONDITIONAL love and forgiveness. We know we can't do it alone, but with your help, we will worry less about what will happen after and focus on your design for forgiveness that brings freedom. We thank you in advance. In the Name of Jesus. Amen.*

There is more that I could say here, but I believe He heard our prayer. Let's *turn the page*!

7 Days to Forgive Them

*7 Days to Forgive Them*

# Blueprint Level 13

a) 9 In this manner, therefore, pray: Our Father in heaven, Hallowed be Your name. 10 Your kingdom come. Your will be done On earth as it is in heaven. 11 Give us this day our daily bread. *12 And forgive us our debts, As we forgive our debtors.* 13 And do not lead us into temptation, But deliver us from the evil one. For Yours is the kingdom and the power and the glory forever. Amen. 14 "For if you forgive men their trespasses, your heavenly Father will also forgive you. 15 But if you do not forgive men their trespasses, neither will your Father forgive your trespasses.

b) Jesus instructs His disciples, "*And when ye stand praying, forgive, if ye have ought against any: that your Father also which is in heaven may forgive you your trespasses. But if ye do not forgive, neither will your Father which is in heaven forgive your trespasses.* "

Key Verses:

    a) Matthew 6:12

    b) Mark 11:25-26

## Excavation

The Disciples Prayer in *Matthew 6* (specifically) and Christ's teachings (in general) explicitly state that God will forgive in the same manner we forgive those who do wrong to us. Jesus, the Christ does not simply provide a prayer example, He TEACHES on forgiveness and HOW it looks in everyday life. He also gives the weight of forgiveness as it relates to our relationship with our Heavenly Father. This was so deeply convicting to me at first, but as I begin to wash my life with this and understand God's grace, it became easier to apply to my hurt and receive the healing and freedom of forgiving others. Again, Christ admonishes us to forgive *so that* we may be forgiven, commanding a condition to our own forgiveness. We know that Jesus, the Christ took forgiveness seriously – so much so that one of His last utterances was "Forgive Them". It is critical that we remember that forgiveness is not for the other person, forgiveness is for US. If we stop thinking that we are "letting them get away" and instead think of it as us getting free, we can do it more easily.

## Foundation Strategy

Today, let's drop off some baggage at the Master's feet. Now, we already know that forgiveness is serious business and we've spent 12 days so far practicing. Today, we just stop and drop. There is a weight that comes with Unforgiveness and quite frankly, it's time to let whatever it is GO. GO – like Get Over (it). Even if it happened last night, the Bible declares that we should not let the sun go down on our wrath. Ready? Let's pray: *Father God, There is a tremendous weight of unforgiving baggage that we need to unload. You said that Your Yoke is easy and Your burden is light, so we seek to trade. Lord, we seek to trade our unrighteous unforgiveness with your righteous judgment of all things past, present and future. You knew it was going to happen and You allowed it and so we ask that you would take it away: the pain, the guilt, the EVERYTHING about it and replace it with Your love, joy, longsuffering, patience, kindness and forgiveness. We thank you in advance for the light load of love that will see us to the end. In The Name of Jesus. Amen.*

Now, you know what I'm going to tell you to do...*turn the page*!

*7 Days to Forgive Them*

*7 Days to Forgive Them*

## Blueprint Level 14

a) To me [God] belongeth vengeance, and recompense: their foot shall hide in due time: for the day of their calamity is at hand, and the things that shall come upon them make haste.

b) Do not touch my anointed ones; do my prophets no harm.

c) Do not touch my anointed ones; do my prophets no harm.

### Key Verses:
a) Deuteronomy 32:35, KJV [my emphasis]
b) 1 Chronicles 16:22, NIV
c) Psalm 105:15, NIV

## Excavation

Three different Scriptures. Three different authors. Three different contextual and historical backgrounds. SAME MESSAGE. That's the part I really want to end these seven days on: God does not change and has not changed His mind. We have 66 Books worth of God's intricately woven and eternally detailed instructions and quite frankly the entire Scripture is about FORGIVENESS. The Fall of Mankind, God's Purpose of Grace, God's Plan of Salvation through forgiveness of our sins. These specific Scriptures are a Segway into our next seven days, but they give us a Key. We do not have to mete out "justice" – it is inherent in God's plan and command to forgive. In simple terms, God is saying: I got you and I got this, so keep moving forward. It may not be immediate and it may not be what you would do, but I have this wrong done unto you under control. If we tell the truth, sometimes, we can actually see God's hands in the worst of those times.

## Foundation Strategy

Today, let's think about how God considers us His anointed. He considers us to be His children. He considers us to be valuable. So much so that He inspired His Word to be written and He sent His Son to die for us – for our FORGIVENESS. He made sure that He ensured that we knew He would take full responsibility for vengeance, repayment, pay back, justice...and even if you do not believe it, I am a living witness, first hand witness, that God will definitely do what He says in His Word. Let's Pray: *Father God, We come to you today in FAITH, believing that You cannot lie and that what you said in Your Word about vengeance is the truth. We release the control that we desire over those who have wronged us back to YOU. We ask that you infuse us with*

Your loving care and peace that You alone have it all under control. In the Name of Jesus. Amen.

There is actually power and liberation in letting someone else do something FOR you. Now, *turn the page* on vengeance!

# 7 Days to Forgive Them

# 7 Days to Forgive Them

# 7 Days to Forget and Flourish

*"To be blessed and highly favored of the Lord, you must PONDER..."*

*L. Chanel*

## Blueprint Level 15

Brothers and sisters, I do not consider myself yet to have taken hold of it. But one thing I do: *Forgetting what is behind and straining toward what is ahead,*

Key Verse: Philippians 3:13

Let me say right up front that I'm only going to spend 2 days on "Forgetting". As I discussed in **The Drama FREE Blueprint:** *Keys to Coming Straight Outta DRAMA*, it's not something that humans can really DO, it's more closely related to something that you have to learn and apply to every day of your life. I believe God has a distinct measure of GRACE for everything that He requires us to do to fill in the gaps. Flourishing, prospering, being successful is both learned behavior AND difficult to do IF you do not master forgiveness. I pray that the first 14 Blueprint Levels have helped you towards your mastery. It's deeper than just forgiving, the blessing comes from being OBEDIENT to God's desire for us to forgive. God highly honors obedience. He says in *1 Samuel* that obedience is better than sacrifice. Obedience brings overflow in areas of your life that you were not even thinking about.

## Excavation

This scripture is one of the most quoted when the idea of forgetting is being discussed, but what's really the PRACTICAL APPLICATION? Well, let's just ask the *Apostle Paul* who wrote it! Paul is highly educated, well experienced and traveled, spiritual adept. So how could he even propose such a thing as forgetting when the entire Old Testament (to which he was an expert) is about remembering?! Yeah, it blew my mind too! Well, it's easy. ***Sorta.*** You need help though. There is no way to even attempt to forget, with positive effect, without having an experience with Jesus and the help of the Holy Spirit. This forgetting and forgiving is not an outer body experience, but an inner work.

## Foundation Strategy

Today, I have to ask a sobering question. Do you have the Holy Spirit dwelling on the inside of you? Now, before you answer, also think about the fact that the Holy Spirit leads and guides us into ALL TRUTH, convicts us, helps us to obey God's standards even when we personally (in the flesh) want to do something different. If your answer is yes, or you "think" your answer is yes, then you have everything you need to proceed with Forgetting and Flourishing. If, by chance, you answered "NO" or "I don't know", don't be discouraged. The Holy Spirit is a GIFT and so you need only ask for it and receive Him fully as the One whom Jesus, the Christ, sent to help us. Now, let's pray: *Father God, We thank you for the gifts that you have given us, Forgiveness through Jesus, the Christ and the Holy Spirit to help us obey you. We ask that you would quicken the Spirit within us that we would seek to forget and press forward just as Paul did. We know that even if our pressing forward is not perfect that You will honor our desire to achieve it. We thank you now for the negative memory loss that will set us free to live a life of purpose and destiny. In the Name of Jesus. Amen.*

## Blueprint Level 16

a) Thou hast cast all my sins behind thy back

b) Thou wilt cast all their sins into the depths of the sea

c) I will forgive their iniquity, and their sin will I remember no more

d) I, even I, am he that blotteth out thy transgressions

e) As far as the east is from the west, so far hath he removed our transgressions from us

### Key Verses:
a) Isaiah 38:17
b) Micah 7:19
c) Jeremiah 31:34
d) Isaiah 43:25
e) Psalms 103:12

## Excavation

I'll keep shouting this from the mountain top, FORGETTING is not the healthy, human, mental state. Our brains are created to capture, catalog, expand, reason...we are hard wired to remember and yet, we FORGET THINGS. Whether we forget ON PURPOSE or not, we do have the capacity to do what I call "file away" or "mental archival". Now, we also have what I call "total recall" because one incident, one word, one phrase can bring up buried (sometimes not so nice) treasure in the blink of an eye. True forgetting, Godly forgetfulness, has nothing to do with random acts of forgetfulness. God tells us in His Word repeatedly that He PURPOSELY and PURPOSEFULLY forgets. It is His divine wise choice. It can be said that we, who are made in God's image and likeness have that same capacity and that we too must CHOOSE to operate in it. Now, let's be clear, we can "forget" what happened, we can forgive what happened, but the consequences of sin may never leave our lives...and perhaps, in God's Omniscience, that's not such a bad thing. The consequences, even of others, make it real. The consequences, even of others keeps us looking externally (howbeit eternally) for something greater, bigger, more powerful than ourselves to give us hope of better. But one thing for sure, it keeps God out of the humankind mind control business because we retain our freedom to choose (aka, *free will*).

## Foundation Strategy

Today, there is only one thing we need to consider: free will. Free – doesn't cost. Cannot be controlled. Will – divine determination. Mental tenacity. Now, let's flip it: WILL YOU BE FREE? Will you choose to change your perspective about forgiveness? I like the Scripture about casting into the sea. It makes me think of how Jesus chose fishermen as His disciples and taught them how to cast their nets wide and deep – catch everything you can – but don't force it...let them come. Let's pray: *Father God, How wonderful and excellent You are in All the Earth! We are so grateful for your eternal wisdom, knowing that we would not be able to comprehend fully "forgetting", but that You established Your forgetting to cover the gap. Even when we struggle to forget, we know that we can rely on you never going backwards to remember what is covered by the blood of Your Son. We thank You for sending Jesus to be example, prophet and savior to show us the way to true freedom – FORGIVENESS AND FORGETTING. We thank you even for the wisdom of Christ that He gave our analytical brains a number - "7 times 70" – and that you meant this to be per day, per person[8]. In the Name of Jesus. Amen.*

---

[8]*Then Peter came to Him and said, "Lord, how often shall my brother sin against me, and I forgive him? Up to seven times?" Jesus said to him, "I do not say to you, up to seven times, but up to seventy times seven. (Matthew 18:21-22)*

*7 Days to Forget and Flourish*

*7 Days to Forget and Flourish*

## Blueprint Level 17

4 Jonathan son of Saul had a son who was lame in both feet. He was five years old when the news about Saul and Jonathan came from Jezreel. His nurse picked him up and fled, but as she hurried to leave, he fell and became disabled. *His name was Mephibosheth.*
2 Samuel 4:4, NIV

*1 Now David said, "Is there still anyone who is left of the house of Saul, that I may show him kindness for Jonathan's sake?"* 2 And there was a servant of the house of Saul whose name was Ziba. So when they had called him to David, the king said to him, "Are you Ziba?" And he said, "At your service!" 3 Then the king said, "Is there not still someone of the house of Saul, to whom I may show the kindness of God?" And Ziba said to the king, "There is still a son of Jonathan who is lame in his feet." 4 So the king said to him, "Where is he?" And Ziba said to the king, "Indeed he is in the house of Machir the son of Ammiel, in Lo Debar." 5 Then King David sent and brought him out of the house of Machir the son of Ammiel, from Lo Debar. 6 Now when Mephibosheth the son of Jonathan, the son of Saul, had come to David, he fell on his face and prostrated himself. Then David said, "Mephibosheth?" And he answered, "Here is your servant!" *7 So David said to him, "Do not fear, for I will surely show you kindness for Jonathan your father's sake, and will restore to you all the land of Saul your grandfather; and you shall eat bread at my table continually."*

Key Verse: 2 Samuel 9:7

## Excavation

Do you really need to keep YOUR word when you make an oath in the midst of a chaotic time in your life? Even if the person who you made the oath to is dead? Even if you genuinely FORGET? Is it possible to FORGET to do something sincere and good? *King David* helps with this. Jonathan was his best friend. He's arguably his only real friend. I say this because he met Jonathan while serving Jonathan's father (*1 Samuel 20 – 2 Samuel 1*[9]); Jonathan's father was King Saul who hated David. DRAMA. When Jonathan was killed, David didn't even really have time to mourn. He had to end his season of being on the run from Jonathan's father, King Saul. He had to deal with those loyal to Saul who wanted him dead. Yet once David becomes king, he remembers...which tells me that he had, for a period of time FORGOTTEN. He remembers that he had not kept his promise to Jonathan. Here's an example of where you can truly *forget* for a season. God will give you grace to forget, even some of the good that happened during a period of your life, to protect your present. David was busy becoming king, bringing the Ark of the Covenant back to the kingdom and hearing the instructions from God for his life and then, he *remembered* that he needed to bless Jonathan's seed. He had been graced with forgetfulness so he could focus! Then, when it was safe, he remembered and took immediate action. There will be times where the Lord will give you that grace to forget. I know He's done it in my life many times. Then, when it's safe for you (physically, emotionally, spiritually), you will remember and do what's right to bring closure to the situation and set yourself free. Don't find yourself in a place of "what if" instead of "it is

---

[9] *7 The king spared Mephibosheth son of Jonathan, the son of Saul, because of the oath before the LORD between David and Jonathan son of Saul.* (**2 Samuel 21:7, NIV**)

finished". Remember when we talked about genealogies and sins of the father being passed down? This is a good reference point. Mephibosheth was born into the royal family at the wrong time, got dropped by the wrong nurse and lived in squalor until...another King remembered. The Key? What God has for you is for you!

## Foundation Strategy

Today, let's focus on the forgiveness that brings CLOSURE. Something negative may occurred and the Lord graced us with forgetfulness, but now it's time to remember to finish the perfect work. Forgiveness means putting the person that wronged us back in the same position to, if they so choose, do it to us again. This is the "turn the other cheek that Jesus teaches about. You've only got two cheeks on your face so at some point, you will be back to the originally slapped cheek! You cannot stand there rubbing your cheek or you will never turn. Now, let's pray:

*Father God, You alone know how to balance remembering with forgetting. You alone are just in all Your ways and yet You call us to be like you. We ask you know to help us to remember to keep our word regardless of the circumstances. We thank you for the grace to forget for seasons to protect us. We ask that You give us the courage to do what is right even when we have been done wrong. In the Name of Jesus. Amen.*

As you recall the things that you intended to do, the things that you gave an oath to do, write them down. If it's possible, do them and receive the freedom of CLOSURE and healing.

*7 Days to Forget and Flourish*

## Blueprint Level 18

...if My people who are called by My name will humble themselves, and pray and seek My face, and turn from their wicked ways, then I will hear from heaven, and will forgive their sin and heal their land
*2 Chronicles 7:14*

30 And may You hear the supplication of Your servant and of Your people Israel, when they pray toward this place. Hear in heaven Your dwelling place; and when You hear, forgive. 31 "When anyone sins against his neighbor, and is forced to take an oath, and comes and takes an oath before Your altar in this temple, 32 then hear in heaven, and act, and judge Your servants, condemning the wicked, bringing his way on his head, and justifying the righteous by giving him according to his righteousness. 33 "When Your people Israel are defeated before an enemy because they have sinned against You, and when they turn back to You and confess Your name, and pray and make supplication to You in this temple, **34 then hear in heaven, and forgive the sin of Your people Israel, and bring them back to the land which You gave to their fathers.** 35 "When the heavens are shut up and there is no rain because they have sinned against You, when they pray toward this place and confess Your name, and turn from their sin because You afflict them, **36 then hear in heaven, and forgive the sin of Your servants, Your people Israel, that You may teach them the good way in which they should walk; and send rain on Your land which You have given to Your people as an inheritance.** 37 "When there is famine in the land, pestilence or blight or mildew, locusts or grasshoppers; when their enemy besieges them in the land of their cities; whatever plague or whatever sickness there is; 38 whatever prayer, whatever supplication is made by anyone, or by all Your people Israel, when each one knows the plague of his own heart, and spreads out his hands toward this temple: **39 then hear in heaven Your dwelling place, and forgive, and act, and give to everyone according to all his ways, whose heart You know (for You alone know the hearts of all the sons of men),**

*Key Verses:*
1 Kings 8:30[ix]; 34; 36; 39

## Excavation

Remember we talked about *King Solomon* in Blueprint Levels 4 and 6? There's even MORE to the story. I almost want to preach right here! Listen, after the prayers and following the instructions, God gives a critical "by product" of forgiveness: <u>HEALING</u>. Forgiveness brings wisdom, and it also brings <u>HEALING</u>. This healing is not just for you because you forgave or for the other person because you forgave, but it has the power to heal an entire nation, an entire family, an entire neighborhood. I think you get the point. Power with purpose can go a long way and it can set a completely different course for your life and everyone else around you. This is how you FLOURISH! There is no way that two things that are diametrically opposed can exist in the same place at the same time, so if you choose to forgive and forget, you will not remember the negative, but instead be healed and renewed by the positive. King Solomon was the wealthiest king AND the wisest man to ever live used both of those resources to solicit the forgiveness of God for the sake of an entire nation. Let us be like him that we want the forgiveness that brings FREEDOM and healing, not just to ourselves, but to anyone in our lives!

## Foundation Strategy

Today, I want you to think about all – as many as you can – the people that are attached to your UNFORGIVENESS of YOU. I know, I know, but trust me, there are people who are depending on you to forgive yourself and heal so that you can help them do the same. This is something I personally know to be true because I am typing these words, I am seeking to live my life according to these words so that you reading this and others will come to do that very same thing. That's exactly what we talked about in Blueprint Level 16, keeping an *oath* of forgiveness. Again, I'll say, it's NOT EASY, but it is so worth it! Let's pray:

*Father God, I want my healing and I know that you want me healed so today, I confess the unforgiveness that I had for myself and ask you to infuse me with your love and forgiveness and heal me from all the thoughts, emotions, relationships and even visible, real scars that are hindering my SELF forgiveness. In the Name of Jesus, Amen.*

That's it. Now, go look in a mirror (or your phone) and say "[**insert your name**] you are FORGIVEN and you are HEALED!" You can journal here about your self-forgiveness affirmation.

*7 Days to Forget and Flourish*

## Blueprint Level 19

But whoever looks intently into the perfect law that gives freedom, and continues in it—**not forgetting** what they have heard, but doing it—they will be blessed in what they do.

Key Verse: James 1:25, NIV

## Excavation

Wait, but you just told us to forget...and now you're telling us to NOT forget? Listen, you've been with me this long, so stay with me. Firstly, let's change that to a more *affirmative* way to say it: **Forget the wrong and Remember to Love and Forgive.** Ecclesiastes says there is a time for everything under the sun[10] and surely, there is always time for balance. Ever so delicate but ever so necessary. Flourishing requires balance – between forgetting and not forgetting. It requires the wisdom to know when you are out of balance. Secondly, remember what un-forgiveness has already cost you – time, relationships, peace, answers to your prayers, blessings held up – and decide that it is not worth it. Unforgiveness costs too much and we can't afford it any longer. *James*, in his short but powerful book, is telling us to REMEMBER WHAT WE'VE BEEN TAUGHT and that when we remember what we were taught (about forgiveness), we will be blessed. The *Key* is that we need to always walk in the wisdom of the knowledge of Jesus the Christ and his eternal example of forgiveness – so much so that He even exemplified it while dying on the cross[11].

## Foundation Strategy

Today is the day that we focus on forgiving by remembering the content of all the tests, trials and all the things that we have learned about how to navigate challenges and matriculate through life from Jesus, the Christ. If nothing else,

---

[10] For everything there is a season, and a time for every matter under heaven: [Ecclesiastes 3:1, English Standard Version (ESV)]
[11] And Jesus said, Father, forgive them, for they know not what they do." And they cast lots to divide his garments. [Luke 23:34, ESV]

although He is much more, He is the principal example on forgiveness. His life's mission was to obtain God's forgiveness FOR mankind and to exemplify God's love TO mankind. Let's pray: *Father, we are so grateful for not only sending us your Word, but for sending us a living, breathing example of your love for us. We thank you today for Jesus, who exemplified love, kindness, faithfulness, longsuffering, peace, grace and forgiveness. We ask you now to heal us of every unforgiving thought and every emotion attached to it that we may truly live out what Jesus taught us. We believe you for it now. In the Name of Jesus. Amen.*

Now, take some time and write out how you will ACTIVELY live out a life of forgiveness towards even those who have wronged you – even tried to kill you. And then...*turn the page*!

*7 Days to Forget and Flourish*

*7 Days to Forget and Flourish*

# Blueprint Level 20

He suffered no man to do them wrong: yea, he reproved kings for their sakes, Saying, touch not mine anointed, and do my prophets no harm…

Key Verse: I Chronicles 16:21-22

## Excavation

This text exemplifies God's forgiving POWER. For all His righteousness, God never outdoes Himself when it comes to His love for us. He calls us ANOINTED. Special. Set Apart. He forgives us even when we are exclusively wrong and reserving true vengeance and judgement for Himself. I don't know about you, but that takes a tremendous weight off of my mind and heart, knowing that I don't have to worry about "wrongful conviction"! If God is truly Omniscient (All Knowing), Omnipresent (Everywhere At the Same Time) and Omnipotent (All powerful) and He chooses to forgive us, when He could just as easily destroy us; we have to believe that He has the power to make our healing complete and favor our lives to fulfillment. I did not say HAPPINESS. Flourishing is about being fully content with the state of your life and living the life you have to its fullest potential IN God. A life of PURPOSE. A life of PASSION. A life of PRODUCTIVITY. Now, I can't speak to what your life will look like outside of God, but I can say that if you ever choose to really forgive, and really ask God to help you forget through Jesus Christ's blood, you will live a flourishing life.

## Foundation Strategy

Today, I want you think about where you thought you might be at this point in your life. **Seriously**. These thoughts are about the potential and ambition of your life. Now, I want you to think about everything we've covered so far and all the affirmations we've declared and process through this *Romans 8:28. ALL things work together for GOOD to them who love God and are called according to HIS purpose.* That's such a liberating Scripture, but it's also packed with instructions. **First** you must love God and **next** you must be called and **finally** you need to be operating in His purpose for your life. It's not as easy as it sounds and it's not as simple as one verse. Some never achieve even the first part – loving God – and that's the most transformational piece. Let's pray:

*Father God, You are LOVE. Your Word repeatedly tells us that you love us unconditionally, but that Your standards must be met. You change not, you fail not, and you never cease to love us. We ask that you would come to our assistance today, help us to love You back! Oh Lord, help us to operate in that same agape love that you have for us and show us Your divine hand in all that we do and say to ourselves through affirmations and to others. We thank You for never giving up on us, or your purpose IN us and we seek to see it fulfilled in our lives. Lord, help us to operate in steadfast, unconditional love that we would live a life of freedom. Bless everything that we touch so that everyone will know that our God is a Great and Mighty God! In the Name of Jesus. Amen.*

Now, listen, this may be the end of we may be nearing the end of this journey, but we are just getting started living lives of peace and freedom through constant, consistent forgiveness that brings flourishing!

**Turn that page!**

*7 Days to Forget and Flourish*

# Blueprint Level 21

## Jesus forgives his enemies

26 As the soldiers led him away, they seized Simon from Cyrene, who was on his way in from the country, and put the cross on him and made him carry it behind Jesus. 27 A large number of people followed him, including women who mourned and wailed for him. 28 Jesus turned and said to them, "Daughters of Jerusalem, do not weep for me; weep for yourselves and for your children. 29 For the time will come when you will say, 'Blessed are the childless women, the wombs that never bore and the breasts that never nursed!' 30 Then they will say to the mountains, "Fall on us!" and to the hills, "Cover us!" ' 31 For if people do these things when the tree is green, what will happen when it is dry?" 32 Two other men, both criminals, were also led out with him to be executed. 33 When they came to the place called the Skull, they crucified him there, along with the criminals—one on his right, the other on his left. *34 Jesus said, Father, forgive them, for they do not know what they are doing."*

And they divided up his clothes by casting lots. 35 The people stood watching, and the rulers even sneered at him. They said, "He saved others; let him save himself if he is God's Messiah, the Chosen One." 36 The soldiers also came up and mocked him. They offered him wine vinegar 37 and said, "If you are the king of the Jews, save yourself." 38 There was a written notice above him, which read: THIS IS THE KING OF THE JEWS. 39 One of the criminals who hung there hurled insults at him: "Aren't you the Messiah? Save yourself and us!" 40 But the other criminal rebuked him. "Don't you fear God," he said, "since you are under the same sentence? 41 We are punished justly, for we are getting what our deeds deserve. But this man has done nothing wrong." 42 Then he said, "Jesus, remember me when you come into your kingdom. 43 Jesus answered him, "Truly I tell you, today you will be with me in paradise."

Key Verses: Luke 23:34; 42-43

## Excavation

This is the perfect conclusion to the whole matter. Here it is, *Jesus*, of Nazareth, the Carpenter, the Prophet, the Miracle Worker, the Teacher, the Son of the Eternal Living God is the only real example we need, although we have so many others. The first *Key* here is that forgiveness requires ACTION and that action will give us tremendous strength and power. In *Luke 23:24*, *Christ* himself exemplified Scripture in ACTION. He shows us what he teaches us in the other gospels; that even when you are facing unjust people who are literally (or virtually) killing you, the only way to think about them is in the spirit of forgiveness. While He is dying a gruesome death, barely able to breathe, He uses one of those last breaths to show that forgiveness is possible and required even unto death. We can never escape the commandment to forgive and we can never undo the freedom, peace and POWER it provides. This is the ultimate purpose of the Holy Scripture – SALVATION from eternal death through forgiveness of our sin. That is why FORGIVENESS has so much POWER. It was wrought by Jesus, the Christ, on the Cross of Calvary. And this is why the enemy fights us so hard on operating IN it!

The other *Key* I want to point out here is that there is no recipe for forgiveness. It will look different every time you see it in action. The *thief on the cross* shows us this. He doesn't have the time, the breath or the knowledge of asking the savior for forgiveness of his sins – it's still a new concept. But what he is able to acknowledge and ask for is to be REMEMBERED by Jesus. Now, that is a huge lesson on discernment and atonement, but just know that while we are striving to forgive and forget, it's all for the sake of being REMEMBERED by the Savior!

## Foundation Strategy

On this last day of the forgiveness challenge, I want us to celebrate the progress made. Just like the cross is a symbol of the finished work of forgiveness, this journey is the finished work of your effort and openness to living a transformed life of freedom. This is not to be taken lightly. People die in their **unforgiveness** every day. Families are split up right now because of **unforgiveness**. Children are mistreated daily due to parental **unforgiveness**. The hospitals are full of sick people who are hoping to be forgiven and wishing they could forgive so that they could be healed in their SOULS. As I said at the onset, forgiveness is REAL and it's achievable in every facet of life. My prayer is that you have learned the principles of practical application and formed the HABIT that will ensure your HEALING and solidify your FREEDOM to live a life of abundant blessings and peace.

Let me seal this time together with a prayer:

*Father God,*

*You are so Awesome and Wondrous! You are Excellent in All the Earth! There is none like you and I magnify Your Holy Name today! Your children have come to Your throne, seeking Your face and needing Your grace for this journey through life as a FORGIVING people. We desire to be more and more like You. We ask that you would now seal this teaching, these revelations, these practical instructions about your principle of FORGIVENESS into our hearts and minds. Whatever you did during these 21 days, make it a lasting covenant and a way of life for us until we meet You face to face. We are so grateful that Your love for us knows no bounds and that You sent Your Son to save us, that you would forgive us that we would learn Your ways and forgive OTHERS. Let not one word of these 21 days fall on fallow ground, but instead, take root and grow into a Sycamore Tree of blessings!*

*In the Name of Jesus. Amen.*

*7 Days to Forget and Flourish*

# Forgive, Forget & Flourish: Certificate of Completion

You have sacrificed 21 days of going down a path of operating daily and consistently in FORGIVENESS. But how do you KNOW that you've been transformed? How do you KNOW if you went beyond reading words on a page, to being purposed about living FREE from DRAMA by operating in FORGIVENESS? Simple: What do you think? Yep, it's really that simple because the Word of God says it's that simple: "*And do not be conformed to this world, but be <u>transformed</u> by the renewing of your mind, that you may prove what is that good and acceptable and perfect will of God*". (Romans 12:2, NKJV)". Here's that same Scripture in the Message translation:

> *Don't become so well-adjusted to your culture that you fit into it without even thinking. Instead, fix your attention on God. You'll be changed from the inside out. Readily recognize what he wants from you, and quickly respond to it. Unlike the culture around you, always dragging you down to its level of immaturity, God brings the best out of you, develops well-formed maturity in you.*

I'm sorry if you thought I had a secret psychological dissertation. I simply trust and rely on the truth and the power of the Scriptures! So, if you find yourself going backwards in your THOUGHTS, guess what?! You have your own words that you've written in this journal, and that you have recited as affirmations and prayers, in addition to the Word of God, to put you back on the straight path to DRAMA FREE! *Here's your certificate – Write your name and walk in your freedom.*

---

*Certificate of Completion*

This award is given to

_____

for successfully completing the devotional journal journey
**21 Days To Free**

*L. Chanel*

L. CHANEL THOMPSON
Lifestyle Blueprint Architect &
CEO of L. Chanel INK

One more thing before I leave you for real, now that you have completed this journey of devotional journaling about forgiveness, may I ask that you please take a few moments to leave a review at https://lchanelink.biz/product/21-days-to-free/.

*Thanks so much and walk free, live free, BE FREE!*

*Extra Journal Pages*
*Continuing To Forgive, Forget & Flourish*

*Extra Journal Pages*

Extra Journal Pages

*Extra Journal Pages*

*Extra Journal Pages*

# Extra Journal Pages

*Extra Journal Pages*

*Extra Journal Pages*

*Extra Journal Pages*

*Extra Journal Pages*

*Extra Journal Pages*

# Extra Journal Pages

*Extra Journal Pages*

*Extra Journal Pages*

*Extra Journal Pages*

*Extra Journal Pages*

*Extra Journal Pages*

*Extra Journal Pages*

*Extra Journal Pages*

*Extra Journal Pages*

*Extra Journal Pages*

*Extra Journal Pages*

*Extra Journal Pages*

*Extra Journal Pages*

*Extra Journal Pages*

*Extra Journal Pages*

*Extra Journal Pages*

*Extra Journal Pages*

*Extra Journal Pages*

*Extra Journal Pages*

*Extra Journal Pages*

*Extra Journal Pages*

*Extra Journal Pages*

*Extra Journal Pages*

*Extra Journal Pages*

*Extra Journal Pages*

*Extra Journal Pages*

*Extra Journal Pages*

*Extra Journal Pages*

*Extra Journal Pages*

*Extra Journal Pages*

# Extra Journal Pages

*Extra Journal Pages*

*Extra Journal Pages*

*Extra Journal Pages*

*Extra Journal Pages*

*Extra Journal Pages*

*Extra Journal Pages*

*Extra Journal Pages*

# Extra Journal Pages

*Extra Journal Pages*

*Extra Journal Pages*

Extra Journal Pages

# Extra Journal Pages

*Extra Journal Pages*

*Extra Journal Pages*

*Extra Journal Pages*

*Extra Journal Pages*

*Extra Journal Pages*

*Extra Journal Pages*

*Extra Journal Pages*

*Extra Journal Pages*

*Extra Journal Pages*

*Extra Journal Pages*

*Extra Journal Pages*

*Extra Journal Pages*

*Extra Journal Pages*

*Extra Journal Pages*

*Extra Journal Pages*

*Extra Journal Pages*

*Extra Journal Pages*

*Extra Journal Pages*

*Extra Journal Pages*

*Extra Journal Pages*

*Extra Journal Pages*

*Extra Journal Pages*

*Extra Journal Pages*

# Extra Journal Pages

*Extra Journal Pages*

*Extra Journal Pages*

*Extra Journal Pages*

# Extra Journal Pages

*Extra Journal Pages*

*Extra Journal Pages*

*Extra Journal Pages*

*Extra Journal Pages*

## About the Author

L. Chanel Thompson is a Minister of the Gospel, Motivational Speaker, Empowerment Coach, Lifestyle Expert and Master Mediator – who happens to love writing and clothes! She channels her infectious energy, jovial spirit, and positive life outlook into empowering men, women and youth through **MiniStreet Evangelism & Global Action (MEGA) Ministries**™ and **L. Chanel INK**™; enabling them to realize and take bold action in identifying and achieving their life's PURPOSE – becoming PURPOSE-FILLED, PRODUCTIVE, POWER Players.

Having professional expertise in writing, teaching, training and project management she is primed to bring all of her resources together to share guidance to young women and men everywhere to help them figure out how to mitigate life's challenges. She couples her special mastery for Program Development with successfully navigating life FREE from DRAMA – *The Life Blueprint Architect*™. With the first installment of The Drama Free Blueprint Series, <u>**The Drama Free Blueprint: Keys to Coming Straight Outta Drama**</u>, she focused on the primary Kingdom Keys to forgiveness. The new companion journal expands on those Kingdom Keys and puts that theme and focus to the test, building a habit of living free from drama through practiced, practical forgiveness in action.

She is following a God-given mandate to make the Bible a relevant 21st century force for the right now, "microwave" generation by "preaching to the streets". Her ministry focuses on the central theme, **"Building A Legacy of Living Free"**, and her audience gets more than just a guide, they get the Word of God and are armed with Truth.

In her own words:

> I wrote The Drama Free Blueprint because in order to build anything, you need a plan – a blueprint – of what "it" will be, where each part of "it" will go, what each piece of "it" will be used for and so on. When I found out that I was going through life without a plan, I knew I had to get one FAST and living in perpetual forgiveness is a key to the plan. This book, this series, is for people like me that truly want to live DRAMA FREE by operating in daily forgiveness and flourishing to live purposed, FULL lives. What's so awesome is that the revelation is so simple that it applies to every part of our life.

Although she absolutely loves writing, fashion, shopping and traveling, her most important jobs are simply Wife of One, Mother of Two and Minister to Whomever the Lord Allows. L. Chanel is excited for the next phase of her life, her career and her purpose.

*Stay Connected with Me*

*Facebook* @LChanelThompson
www.facebook.com/LChanelThompson

*Instagram* @lchanelspeaks
www.instagram.com/LChanelSpeaks

*Twitter* @lchanelspeaks
www.twitter.com/LChanelspeaks

# Endnotes
## Studying to Forgive, Forget & Flourish

# Endnotes

# Endnotes

---

[i] Daniel's Prayer (Daniel 9, **entire prayer for context and future study from the New International Version**)

1 In the first year of Darius son of Xerxes (a Mede by descent), who was made ruler over the Babylonian kingdom— 2 in the first year of his reign, I, Daniel, understood from the Scriptures, according to the word of the LORD given to Jeremiah the prophet, that the desolation of Jerusalem would last seventy years. 3 So I turned to the Lord God and pleaded with him in prayer and petition, in fasting, and in sackcloth and ashes. 4 I prayed to the LORD my God and confessed: "Lord, the great and awesome God, who keeps his covenant of love with those who love him and keep his commandments, 5 we have sinned and done wrong. We have been wicked and have rebelled; we have turned away from your commands and laws. 6 We have not listened to your servants the prophets, who spoke in your name to our kings, our princes and our ancestors, and to all the people of the land. 7 "Lord, you are righteous, but this day we are covered with shame—the people of Judah and the inhabitants of Jerusalem and all Israel, both near and far, in all the countries where you have scattered us because of our unfaithfulness to you. 8 We and our kings, our princes and our ancestors are covered with shame, LORD, because we have sinned against you. 9 The Lord our God is merciful and forgiving, even though we have rebelled against him; 10 we have not obeyed the LORD our God or kept the laws he gave us through his servants the prophets. 11 All Israel has transgressed your law and turned away, refusing to obey you. "Therefore the curses and sworn judgments written in the Law of Moses, the servant of God, have been poured out on us, because we have sinned against you. 12 You have fulfilled the words spoken against us and against our rulers by bringing on us great disaster. Under the whole heaven nothing has ever been done like what has been done to Jerusalem. 13 Just as it is written in the Law of Moses, all this disaster has come on us, yet we have not sought the favor of the LORD our God by turning from our sins and giving attention to your truth. 14 The LORD did not hesitate to bring the disaster on us, for the LORD our God is righteous in everything he does; yet we have not obeyed him. 15 "Now, Lord our God, who brought your people out of Egypt with a mighty hand and who made for yourself a name that endures to this day, we have sinned, we have done wrong. 16 Lord, in keeping with all your righteous acts, turn away your anger and your wrath from Jerusalem, your city, your holy hill. Our sins and the iniquities of our ancestors have made Jerusalem and your people an object of scorn to all those around us. 17 "Now, our God, hear the prayers

and petitions of your servant. For your sake, Lord, look with favor on your desolate sanctuary. 18 Give ear, our God, and hear; open your eyes and see the desolation of the city that bears your Name. We do not make requests of you because we are righteous, but because of your great mercy. *19 Lord, listen! Lord, forgive! Lord, hear and act! For your sake, my God, do not delay, because your city and your people bear your Name."*

ii The Seventy "Sevens" **(Daniel 9, NIV)** 20 While I was speaking and praying, confessing my sin and the sin of my people Israel and making my request to the LORD my God for his holy hill— 21 while I was still in prayer, Gabriel, the man I had seen in the earlier vision, came to me in swift flight about the time of the evening sacrifice. 22 He instructed me and said to me, "Daniel, I have now come to give you insight and understanding. 23 As soon as you began to pray, a word went out, which I have come to tell you, for you are highly esteemed. Therefore, consider the word and understand the vision: 24 "Seventy 'sevens' are decreed for your people and your holy city to finish transgression, to put an end to sin, to atone for wickedness, to bring in everlasting righteousness, to seal up vision and prophecy and to anoint the Most Holy Place. 25 "Know and understand this: From the time the word goes out to restore and rebuild Jerusalem until the Anointed One, the ruler, comes, there will be seven 'sevens,' and sixty-two 'sevens.' It will be rebuilt with streets and a trench, but in times of trouble. 26 After the sixty-two 'sevens,' the Anointed One will be put to death and will have nothing. The people of the ruler who will come will destroy the city and the sanctuary. The end will come like a flood: War will continue until the end, and desolations have been decreed. 27 He will confirm a covenant with many for one 'seven.' In the middle of the 'seven' he will put an end to sacrifice and offering. And at the temple he will set up an abomination that causes desolation, until the end that is decreed is poured out on him.

# Endnotes

[iii] Hezekiah King of Judah **(2 King 18)** 1 In the third year of Hoshea son of Elah king of Israel, Hezekiah son of Ahaz king of Judah began to reign. 2 He was twenty-five years old when he became king, and he reigned in Jerusalem twenty-nine years. His mother's name was Abijah daughter of Zechariah. 3 He did what was right in the eyes of the LORD, just as his father David had done. 4 He removed the high places, smashed the sacred stones and cut down the Asherah poles. He broke into pieces the bronze snake Moses had made, for up to that time the Israelites had been burning incense to it. (It was called Nehushtan.) 5 Hezekiah trusted in the LORD, the God of Israel. There was no one like him among all the kings of Judah, either before him or after him. 6 He held fast to the LORD and did not stop following him; he kept the commands the LORD had given Moses. 7 And the LORD was with him; he was successful in whatever he undertook. He rebelled against the king of Assyria and did not serve him. 8 From watchtower to fortified city, he defeated the Philistines, as far as Gaza and its territory. 9 In King Hezekiah's fourth year, which was the seventh year of Hoshea son of Elah king of Israel, Shalmaneser king of Assyria marched against Samaria and laid siege to it. 10 At the end of three years the Assyrians took it. So Samaria was captured in Hezekiah's sixth year, which was the ninth year of Hoshea king of Israel. **11 The king of Assyria deported Israel to Assyria and settled them in Halah, in Gozan on the Habor River and in towns of the Medes. 12 This happened because they had not obeyed the LORD their God, but had violated his covenant—all that Moses the servant of the LORD commanded. They neither listened to the commands nor carried them out.** 13 In the fourteenth year of King Hezekiah's reign, Sennacherib king of Assyria attacked all the fortified cities of Judah and captured them. 14 So Hezekiah king of Judah sent this message to the king of Assyria at Lachish: "I have done wrong. Withdraw from me, and I will pay whatever you demand of me." The king of Assyria exacted from Hezekiah king of Judah three hundred talents of silver and thirty talents of gold. 15 So Hezekiah gave him all the silver that was found in the temple of the LORD and in the treasuries of the royal palace. **16 At this time Hezekiah king of Judah stripped off the gold with which he had covered the doors and doorposts of the temple of the LORD, and gave it to the king of Assyria.**

[iv] Isaiah Prophesies Sennacherib's Fall **(2 Kings 19)** 20 Then Isaiah son of Amoz sent a

message to Hezekiah: "This is what the LORD, the God of Israel, says: I have heard your prayer concerning Sennacherib king of Assyria. 21 This is the word that the LORD has spoken against him: " 'Virgin Daughter Zion despises you and mocks you. Daughter Jerusalem tosses her head as you flee. 22 Who is it you have ridiculed and blasphemed? Against whom have you raised your voice and lifted your eyes in pride? Against the Holy One of Israel! 23 By your messengers you have ridiculed the Lord. And you have said, "With my many chariots I have ascended the heights of the mountains, the utmost heights of Lebanon. I have cut down its tallest cedars, the choicest of its junipers. I have reached its remotest parts, the finest of its forests. 24 I have dug wells in foreign lands and drunk the water there. With the soles of my feet I have dried up all the streams of Egypt." 25 " 'Have you not heard? Long ago I ordained it. In days of old I planned it; now I have brought it to pass, that you have turned fortified cities into piles of stone. 26 Their people, drained of power, are dismayed and put to shame. They are like plants in the field, like tender green shoots, like grass sprouting on the roof, scorched before it grows up. 27 " 'But I know where you are and when you come and go and how you rage against me. 28 Because you rage against me and because your insolence has reached my ears, I will put my hook in your nose and my bit in your mouth, and I will make you return by the way you came.' 29 "This will be the sign for you, Hezekiah: "This year you will eat what grows by itself, and the second year what springs from that. But in the third year sow and reap, plant vineyards and eat their fruit. 30 Once more a remnant of the kingdom of Judah will take root below and bear fruit above. 31 For out of Jerusalem will come a remnant, and out of Mount Zion a band of survivors. "The zeal of the LORD Almighty will accomplish this. 32 "Therefore this is what the LORD says concerning the king of Assyria: " 'He will not enter this city or shoot an arrow here. He will not come before it with shield or build a siege ramp against it. 33 By the way that he came he will return; he will not enter this city, declares the LORD. 34 I will defend this city and save it, for my sake and for the sake of David my servant.' " 35 That night the angel of the LORD went out and put to death a hundred and eighty-five thousand in the Assyrian camp. When the people got up the next morning—there were all the dead bodies! **36 So Sennacherib king of Assyria broke camp and withdrew. He returned to Nineveh and stayed there. 37 One day, while he was worshiping in the temple of his god Nisrok, his sons Adrammelek and Sharezer killed him with the sword, and they escaped to the land of Ararat. And Esarhaddon his son succeeded him as king.**

[v] You may also want to create a prayer box, with index cards where you keep these things written down and can track your growth and ultimately grow your faith.

[vi] Solomon's Prayer of Dedication **(1 Kings 8, entire prayer for context and future study from the New International Version)** 22 Then Solomon stood before the altar of the LORD in front of the whole assembly of Israel, spread out his hands toward heaven 23 and said: "LORD, the God of Israel, there is no God like you in heaven above or on earth below—you who keep your covenant of love with your servants who continue wholeheartedly in your way. 24 You have kept your promise to your servant David my father; with your mouth you have promised and with your hand you have fulfilled it—as it is today. 25 "Now LORD, the God of Israel, keep for your servant David my father the promises you made to him when you said, 'You shall never fail to have a successor to sit before me on the throne of Israel, if only your descendants are careful in all they do to walk before me faithfully as you have done.' 26 And now, God of Israel, let your word that you promised your servant David my father come true. 27 "But will God really dwell on earth? The heavens, even the highest heaven, cannot contain you. How much less this temple I have built! 28 Yet give attention to your servant's prayer and his plea for mercy, LORD my God. Hear the cry and the prayer that your servant is praying in your presence this day. 29 May your eyes be open toward this temple night and day, this place of which you said, 'My Name shall be there,' so that you will hear the prayer your servant prays toward this place. **30 Hear the supplication of your servant and of your people Israel when they pray toward this place. Hear from heaven, your dwelling place, and when you hear, forgive.** 31 "When anyone wrongs their neighbor and is required to take an oath and they come and swear the oath before your altar in this temple, 32 then hear from heaven and act. Judge between your servants, condemning the guilty by bringing down on their heads what they have done, and vindicating the innocent by treating them in accordance with their innocence. 33 "When your people Israel have been defeated by an enemy because they have sinned against you, and when they turn back to you and give praise to your name, praying and making supplication to you in this temple, 34 then hear from heaven and forgive the sin of your people Israel and bring them back to the land you gave to their ancestors. 35 "When the heavens are shut up and there is no rain because your people have sinned against you, and when they pray toward this place and give praise to your name and turn from their sin because you have afflicted them, 36 then hear from

heaven and forgive the sin of your servants, your people Israel. Teach them the right way to live, and send rain on the land you gave your people for an inheritance. 37 "When famine or plague comes to the land, or blight or mildew, locusts or grasshoppers, or when an enemy besieges them in any of their cities, whatever disaster or disease may come, 38 and when a prayer or plea is made by anyone among your people Israel—being aware of the afflictions of their own hearts, and spreading out their hands toward this temple— 39 then hear from heaven, your dwelling place. Forgive and act; deal with everyone according to all they do, since you know their hearts (for you alone know every human heart), 40 so that they will fear you all the time they live in the land you gave our ancestors. 41 "As for the foreigner who does not belong to your people Israel but has come from a distant land because of your name— 42 for they will hear of your great name and your mighty hand and your outstretched arm—when they come and pray toward this temple, 43 then hear from heaven, your dwelling place. Do whatever the foreigner asks of you, so that all the peoples of the earth may know your name and fear you, as do your own people Israel, and may know that this house I have built bears your Name. 44 "When your people go to war against their enemies, wherever you send them, and when they pray to the LORD toward the city you have chosen and the temple I have built for your Name, 45 then hear from heaven their prayer and their plea, and uphold their cause. 46 "When they sin against you—for there is no one who does not sin—and you become angry with them and give them over to their enemies, who take them captive to their own lands, far away or near; 47 and if they have a change of heart in the land where they are held captive, and repent and plead with you in the land of their captors and say, 'We have sinned, we have done wrong, we have acted wickedly'; 48 and if they turn back to you with all their heart and soul in the land of their enemies who took them captive, and pray to you toward the land you gave their ancestors, toward the city you have chosen and the temple I have built for your Name; 49 then from heaven, your dwelling place, hear their prayer and their plea, and uphold their cause. 50 And forgive your people, who have sinned against you; forgive all the offenses they have committed against you, and cause their captors to show them mercy; 51 for they are your people and your inheritance, whom you brought out of Egypt, out of that iron-smelting furnace. 52 "May your eyes be open to your servant's plea and to the plea of your people Israel, and may you listen to them whenever they cry out to you. 53 For you singled them out from all the nations of the world to be your own inheritance, just as you declared through your servant Moses when you, Sovereign LORD, brought our ancestors out of Egypt." 54 When Solomon had finished all these prayers and supplications to the LORD, he rose from before the altar of the LORD, where he had been kneeling with his hands spread out toward heaven. 55 He stood and blessed the whole assembly of Israel in a loud voice, saying: 56 "Praise be to the LORD, who has given rest to his people Israel just as he promised. Not one word has failed of all the good promises he gave through his servant Moses. 57 May the LORD our God be with us as he was with our ancestors; may he never leave us nor forsake us. 58 May he turn our hearts to him, to walk in obedience to him and keep the commands, decrees and laws he gave our ancestors. 59 And may these words of mine, which I have prayed before the LORD, be near to the LORD our God day and night, that he may uphold the cause of his servant and the cause of his people Israel according to each day's need, 60 so that all the peoples of the earth may know that the LORD is God and that there is no other. 61 And may your hearts be fully committed to the LORD our God, to live by his decrees and obey his commands, as at this time."

[vii] vii **Jeremiah 1:5, NKJV** "Before I formed you in the womb I knew you; Before you were born I sanctified you; I ordained you a prophet to the nations."

[viii] Solomon's Prayer of Dedication **(1 Kings 8, entire prayer for context and future study from the New International Version)** 22 Then Solomon stood before the altar of the LORD in front of the whole assembly of Israel, spread out his hands toward heaven 23 and said: "LORD, the God of Israel, there is no God like you in heaven above or on earth below—you who keep your covenant of love with your servants who continue wholeheartedly in your way. 24 You have kept your promise to your servant David my father; with your mouth you have promised and with your hand you have fulfilled it—as it is today. 25 "Now LORD, the God of Israel, keep for your servant David my father the promises you made to him when you said, 'You shall never fail to have a successor to sit before me on the throne of Israel, if only your descendants are careful in all they do to walk before me faithfully as you have done.' 26 And now, God of Israel, let your word that you promised your servant David my father come true. 27 "But will God really dwell on earth? The heavens, even the highest heaven, cannot contain you. How much less this temple I have built! 28 Yet give attention to your servant's prayer and his plea for mercy, LORD my God. Hear the cry and the prayer that your servant is praying in your presence this

day. 29 May your eyes be open toward this temple night and day, this place of which you said, 'My Name shall be there,' so that you will hear the prayer your servant prays toward this place. 30 Hear the supplication of your servant and of your people Israel when they pray toward this place. Hear from heaven, your dwelling place, and when you hear, forgive. 31 "When anyone wrongs their neighbor and is required to take an oath and they come and swear the oath before your altar in this temple, 32 then hear from heaven and act. Judge between your servants, condemning the guilty by bringing down on their heads what they have done, and vindicating the innocent by treating them in accordance with their innocence. 33 "When your people Israel have been defeated by an enemy because they have sinned against you, and when they turn back to you and give praise to your name, praying and making supplication to you in this temple, 34 then hear from heaven and forgive the sin of your people Israel and bring them back to the land you gave to their ancestors. 35 "When the heavens are shut up and there is no rain because your people have sinned against you, and when they pray toward this place and give praise to your name and turn from their sin because you have afflicted them, 36 then hear from heaven and forgive the sin of your servants, your people Israel. Teach them the right way to live, and send rain on the land you gave your people for an inheritance. 37 "When famine or plague comes to the land, or blight or mildew, locusts or grasshoppers, or when an enemy besieges them in any of their cities, whatever disaster or disease may come, 38and when a prayer or plea is made by anyone among your people Israel—being aware of the afflictions of their own hearts, and spreading out their hands toward this temple— 39then hear from heaven, your dwelling place. Forgive and act; deal with everyone according to all they do, since you know their hearts (for you alone know every human heart), 40 so that they will fear you all the time they live in the land you gave our ancestors. 41 "As for the foreigner who does not belong to your people Israel but has come from a distant land because of your name— 42 for they will hear of your great name and your mighty hand and your outstretched arm—when they come and pray toward this temple, 43 then hear from heaven, your dwelling place. Do whatever the foreigner asks of you, so that all the peoples of the earth may know your name and fear you, as do your own people Israel, and may know that this house I have built bears your Name. 44 "When your people go to war against their enemies, wherever you send them, and when they pray to the LORD toward the city you have chosen and the temple I have built for your Name, 45 then hear from heaven their prayer and their plea, and uphold their cause. 46 "When they sin against you—for there is

# Endnotes

no one who does not sin—and you become angry with them and give them over to their enemies, who take them captive to their own lands, far away or near; 47 and if they have a change of heart in the land where they are held captive, and repent and plead with you in the land of their captors and say, 'We have sinned, we have done wrong, we have acted wickedly'; 48 and if they turn back to you with all their heart and soul in the land of their enemies who took them captive, and pray to you toward the land you gave their ancestors, toward the city you have chosen and the temple I have built for your Name; 49 then from heaven, your dwelling place, hear their prayer and their plea, and uphold their cause. 50 And forgive your people, who have sinned against you; forgive all the offenses they have committed against you, and cause their captors to show them mercy; 51 for they are your people and your inheritance, whom you brought out of Egypt, out of that iron-smelting furnace. 52 "May your eyes be open to your servant's plea and to the plea of your people Israel, and may you listen to them whenever they cry out to you. 53 For you singled them out from all the nations of the world to be your own inheritance, just as you declared through your servant Moses when you, Sovereign LORD, brought our ancestors out of Egypt." 54 When Solomon had finished all these prayers and supplications to the LORD, he rose from before the altar of the LORD, where he had been kneeling with his hands spread out toward heaven. 55 He stood and blessed the whole assembly of Israel in a loud voice, saying: 56 "Praise be to the LORD, who has given rest to his people Israel just as he promised. Not one word has failed of all the good promises he gave through his servant Moses. 57 May the LORD our God be with us as he was with our ancestors; may he never leave us nor forsake us. 58 May he turn our hearts to him, to walk in obedience to him and keep the commands, decrees and laws he gave our ancestors. 59 And may these words of mine, which I have prayed before the LORD, be near to the LORD our God day and night, that he may uphold the cause of his servant and the cause of his people Israel according to each day's need, 60 so that all the peoples of the earth may know that the LORD is God and that there is no other. 61 And may your hearts be fully committed to the LORD our God, to live by his decrees and obey his commands, as at this time."

[ix] All Scriptures are quoted from the New King James Version of the Holy Bible unless otherwise noted.

www.ingramcontent.com/pod-product-compliance
Lightning Source LLC
Chambersburg PA
CBHW080334170426
43194CB00014B/2556